# Delightful Homemade Bath Bomb Book.
# Recipes For All Occasions: Therapeutic Effects, Relaxation, Stress Relief, Romance

## Your Free Gift

I wanted to show my appreciation that you support my work so I've put together a free gift for you.

http://www.olkha.co/gelato.html

**Gelato - Italian-style ice cream cookbook**

Just visit the link above to download it now.

I know you will love this gift.

Thanks!

# Table of contents

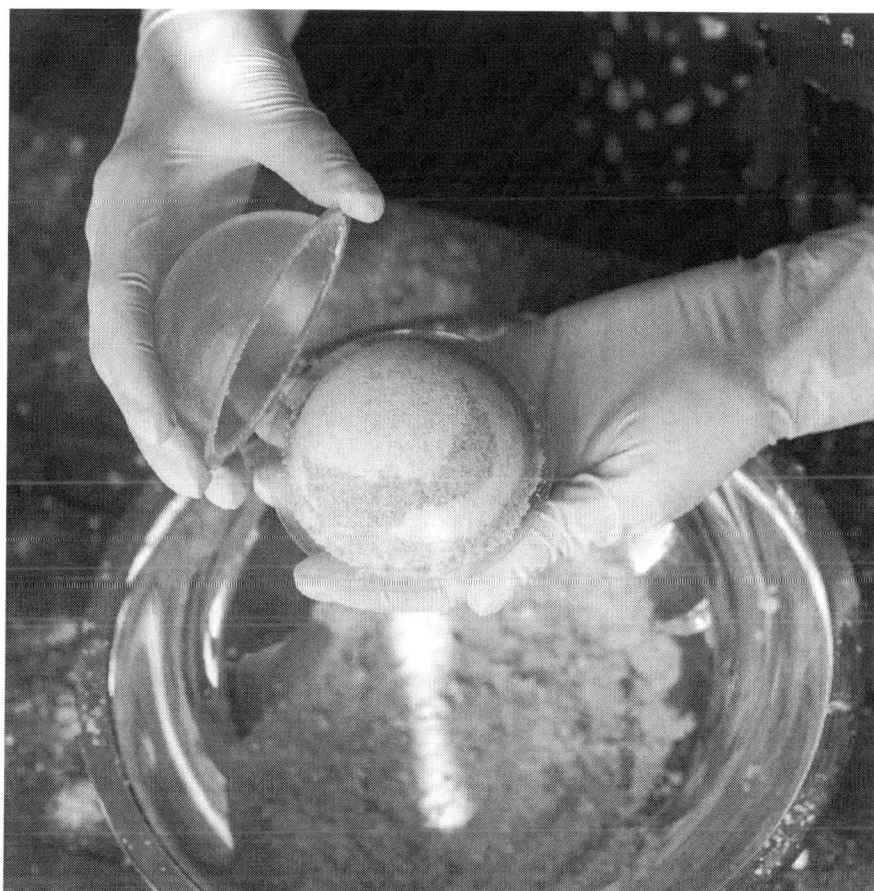

# Relaxing bath bombs

## Herbal tea bath bomb

These bath bombs with herbs can help to make your skin elastic and soft. The mixture of herbs will help to get rid of acne and avoid migraines and insomnia. Use these bath bombs with herbs for your night and evening bath time.

**Ingredients**

1 teaspoon dry calendula
1 teaspoon dry lavender
½ cup baking soda
1 teaspoon rosehip
1 teaspoon rose petals
½ teaspoon essential rose oil
1 teaspoon olive oil
1 teaspoon essential lemon oil
1 teaspoon cinnamon oil
1 cup citric acid
½ cup Epsom salt

**Directions**

Take the big bowl and place the dry calendula, baking soda, dry lavender, rosehip, and rose petals in it. Stir it carefully. Then pour the essential rose oil in the mixture and stir it again. After this, add olive oil, essential lemon oil, and cinnamon oil. Stir it carefully. Then add Epsom salt and mix it till you get a smooth and nice mixture. After this, add citric acid and stir the mixture carefully with the help of a wooden spoon. Then transfer the bath bomb mixture in the special molds and press the mixture tightly. Leave the bath bombs in a warm place for at least 7 hours. Then remove the bath bombs from the molds and keep them in a plastic bag in a dry place.

## Cinnamon bath bomb

The cardamom oil improves appetite, reduces irritability, relieves headaches, coughs, colic, flatulence, dyspepsia, heartburn. It is the best oil to get rid of the overtiredness. The cardamom oil helps to stimulate the growth of hair.

### Ingredients

1/2 cup baking soda
¼ cup oatmeal
½ cup citric acid
½ cup salt
1 teaspoon cardamom oil
1 teaspoon essential ginger oil
1 teaspoon essential cinnamon oil

### Directions

Combine the oatmeal and citric acid together. Stir the mixture gently. Then add salt, baking soda, and essential ginger oil. After this, add essential cinnamon oil and cardamom oil. Whisk the mixture carefully with the help of the hand whisker. When you get a smooth mass – transfer it in the special bath bomb molds or use the muffins forms. Put the mixture in the molds tightly. Then leave the molds with the bath bomb mixture for at least 8 hours in a dry place. When the bath bombs are ready – remove them from the molds and wrap them in plastic bags. You can keep the bath bombs in the bathroom in a dry place.

## Bedtime bath bomb

Using of such bombs in the evening will help you relax. The mixture of the oils will make your skin soft and nourishes it with useful vitamins. The unique aroma of the jasmine oil can bring you the feeling of calmness and create the romantic atmosphere in your bathroom. These bath bombs make you feel better even after the most difficult day and will give you tightly dream.

### Ingredients

1 teaspoon jasmine oil
1/3 cup baking soda
1 teaspoon lavender oil
1 teaspoon jojoba oil
½ cup cornstarch
½ cup citric acid
1 teaspoon Epsom salt

### Directions

Place the jasmine oil, lavender oil, and jojoba oil together in a mixing bowl. Stir the mixture carefully. Then take a separate mixing bowl and place the dry ingredients in it. Stir the mixture carefully. After this put the dry mixture in the liquid mixture and whisk it constantly with the help of the hand whisker. Stop to do it when you get a smooth and nice mixture. Then transfer the mixture in the special bath bombs or use the muffin molds for it. Press the mixture tightly in them. After this, leave the bath bombs for at least 6 hours in a dry place. Then remove the bath bombs from the molds and wrap them in the plastic paper. Keep the bath bombs in the cupboard bags or in the bath room in a dry place.

# Anti-insomnia bath bomb

These bath bombs contain a mix of oils that can get rid of your insomnia and tiredness. The pine essential oil will help you to prevent running noise and bronchitis. Dry calendula is an antibacterial agent. It is effective in the treatment of dermatitis, eczema, acne, sores, wounds, bruises, minor infections or fungal infections, insect bites or jellyfish stings, gastritis with ulcers, minor burns, conjunctivitis, periodontal disease or gingivitis, and sore throat.

## Ingredients

1 teaspoon pine essential oil
½ teaspoon cinnamon oil
1 teaspoon olive oil
1 teaspoon dry calendula
½ cup cornstarch
½ cup citric acid
1/3 cup salt
½ cup baking soda

## Direction

Combine the pine essential oil and cinnamon oil together and whisk the mixture. Then add olive oil and cornstarch. Stir the mixture carefully and add salt. Churn the mixture carefully. When you get a nice mixture – add citric acid and baking soda. Stir the mixture with the help of a wooden spoon. Then take the special bath bomb molds and put the mixture in it tightly. Press them a little. Then remove the bath bombs from the molds and leave the bath bombs in a dry place for 5 hours. After this, wrap the bath bombs in plastic bags and keep them in a dry place.

## Relaxation bath bomb

The essential bergamot oil is used as an antispasmodic, sedative, anti-inflammatory agent. It is possible to use the oil for massage and as an antiseptic. Bergamot oil helps to normalize the secretion of the sebaceous and sweat glands; it has the ability to narrow the pores of the skin.

### Ingredients

½ cup baking soda
1 teaspoon essential bergamot oil
1 teaspoon lavender oil
1 teaspoon cream of tartar
1 cup salt
1 cup citric acid
1 teaspoon dry lavender

### Directions

Combine the salt, baking soda, and citric acid in a mixing bowl. Add cream of tartar and stir it. Then add dry lavender. Take a separate bowl and combine the lavender oil and essential bergamot together in it. Whisk the mixture. Then pour the oil liquid in the dry mixture very slowly. Whisk it constantly. When you get a nice mixture – form it into balls. Transfer the bath bomb balls into the special molds and press them tightly. Leave the mixture for at least 5 hours. Then remove the bombs from the molds and wrap them in the wrapping paper. Keep the bath bombs in a dry place. Do not keep the bath bombs in the bathroom.

# Jasmine bath bomb

Jasmine oil is the best remedy for your skin. It will help you to get rid of the pessimistic thought. Jasmine essential oil perfectly works on all skin types. The main feature of the oil is a moisturizing effect. The best time to use the jasmine oil is night or evening. The bath bombs with this oil will not only make you feel calm but also will give you the aroma of love and happiness.

## Ingredients

1 teaspoon jasmine essential oil
1 teaspoon olive oil
½ teaspoon almond oil
½ cup salt
½ cup citric acid
1 teaspoon dry chamomile
1/3 cup baking soda

## Directions

Take the big mixing bowl and combine the salt, baking soda and citric acid together. Then add olive oil and almond oil. Take the hand mixer and start to mix the mixture till you get a slightly wet mixture. After this take the bath bomb molds and put the dry chamomile in every mold. Then transfer the dry mixture into it. Press the bath bombs and leave them for at least 6 hours in a dry place. Then remove the bombs from the molds very carefully to not damage it. Keep the bath bombs in the cupboard bags in a dry place.

# Peppermint bath bomb

Peppermint bath bomb is the best remedy if you have a headache. It has a positive influence on your heart system. The essential peppermint oil has the soothing influence on the skin and relieves irritation and fatigue, and it can narrow capillaries.

## Ingredients

1 teaspoon dry peppermint
1 teaspoon essential peppermint oil
1 teaspoon olive oil
½ teaspoon jasmine oil
1 cup citric acid
½ cup salt
2 tablespoon cornstarch
½ cup baking soda

## Directions

Take the mixing bowl and combine the olive oil, jasmine oil, and the essential peppermint oil in it. Whisk it carefully with the help of the hand whisker. Then add dry peppermint and stir it gently. Take the second bowl and put citric acid, baking soda, and salt in it. After this, add cornstarch and stir it gently. Then combine the dry mixture and liquid mixture together. Stir it carefully with the help of the fork. When you get a smooth mixture – transfer it in the bath bomb forms and press it tightly. Leave it for 6 hours. Then remove the bath bombs from the forms and use it. Keep the bath bombs in plastic bags in a dry place.

# Rose petals bomb

Essential rose oil has the good influence on the skin; it rejuvenates, makes smooth the fine lines, and improves its firmness and elasticity. Also, such oil regulates the sebaceous glands, eliminates irritation and flaking. Using the bath bombs with essential rose oil will make your skin healthy and beautiful.

## Ingredients

1 tablespoon dry rose petals
1 teaspoon essential rose oil
1 teaspoon coconut oil
½ cup citric acid
¼ cup salt
1 tablespoon cornstarch
½ cup baking soda

## Directions

Combine the citric acid, salt, baking soda, and cornstarch together in a mixing bowl. After this, add dry rose petals in the mixture. Then pour the essential rose oil slowly in the mixture. Stir it constantly. Then add coconut oil and stir the mixture carefully till you get a nice mixture. When the bath bomb mixture is done – transfer it in the special bath bomb molds and leave the bath bombs for / hours or overnight in warm and dry place. When the time is over – remove the bath bombs from the molds and wrap it in the paper bags. Keep in a warm and dry place. Do not keep in the bathroom.

# Chamomile bath bomb

Chamomile bath bomb is a great solution for nighttime bath. Chamomile has great relaxing feature. Such bath bomb will make your mind calm and give you an easy way to feel asleep. The connection of chamomile oil and dry chamomile will help to keep your skin in a shape.

**Ingredients**

¼ cup baking soda
1/3 cup citric acid
1 tablespoon chamomile oil
1 tablespoon dry chamomile
1 tablespoon oatmeal
½ teaspoon olive oil

**Directions**

Take the big mixing bowl and put the baking soda and citric acid in it. Stir it gently and add the teaspoon of the oatmeal. Stir the mixture carefully. Then take a separate mixing bowl and combine olive oil and chamomile oil in it. Whisk the mass. Add oatmeal and stir it carefully again. Then pour the liquid mixture into the dry mixture very slowly. Stir it constantly with the help of the spoon. When you have nice mixture – transfer the mixture in the molds and leave it in adry place for 7 hours. Use it.
Keep the bath bombs in a dry place and the cardboard box.

# Vanilla bath bomb

Vanilla oil is used to treat burns and wounds on the skin, heals various injuries. The ethereal vanilla essence whitens the skin, makes the complexion more even, relieves irritation and eliminates the rash, soothes, relaxes, improves skin elasticity, removes greasy shine and moisturizes.

Vanilla is a good source of vitamins of group B, including thiamine, niacin, pantothenic acid and vitamin B6. All these compounds play an important role in the maintaining of the skin health.

## Ingredients

1 vanilla pod
½ cup baking soda
1 teaspoon vanilla extract
1 tablespoon coconut oil
½ cup citric acid
1/3 cup salt
1/5 cup starch

## Directions

Take the vanilla pod and blend it with the help of the blender. Then combine the blended vanilla pod with the vanilla extract. Stir the mixture. Take a separate bowl and combine the citric acid, baking soda and salt. Stir the mixture. Add starch and stir it again. Then pour the vanilla liquid mixture in the dry mixture very slowly. Stir it constantly. When you get a smooth mixture – transfer the bath bomb mixture in the special bath bomb mold. Press it tightly and leave the bath bomb for at least 5 hours. Then remove the bath bombs from the molds. The bath bombs are ready to use.

Keep in a dry place in the cupboard bags.

# Lavender bath bomb

Lavender is the best way to avoid a headache. The bath bombs with lavender can help you to feel better if you have a sore throat, cough or just feel bad because of the cold weather. It is the best solution if you have insomnia. Use the lavender bath bombs for the evening time bath.

## Ingredients

1 teaspoon lavender essential oil
1 tablespoon dry lavender
1/3 cup baking soda
¼ cup citric acid
½ teaspoon glycerin
1 tablespoon oatmeal

## Directions

Take the big bowl and combine the dry lavender, baking soda, glycerin, and oatmeal in it. Stir the mixture till you get a nice mixture. Then add lavender essential oil very slowly. Stir it again till you get a smooth mass. Then take the molds for the bath bombs and transfer the mixture to them. Put the mixture in the molds very tightly. Then put the press on the bombs and leave them for 5 hours. After this, remove the bath bombs from the molds and use it. Keep the lavender bath bombs in a dry place, not in the bathroom. Use the cupboard bag for the bombs to save the aromatic features of it.

# Green tea bath bomb

Tea tree oil is one of the most famous oils that are used in the cosmetology. It has numerous of the helpful features for our body. The tea tree oil quickly restores of the skin; it has a strong regenerative effect and relieves skin irritation, redness, inflammation, and swelling. Aromatic properties of natural tea tree oil have also an active protective effect on human bioenergetics and help maintain calm of your mind and focus on the most challenging situations.

## Ingredients

3 tablespoon cornstarch
1/3 cup baking soda
¼ cup citric acid
1 tablespoon dry green tea leaves
1 teaspoon tea tree oil
1 teaspoon olive oil
½ tablespoon almond oil

## Directions

Take the big mixing bowl and combine the cornstarch, baking soda and citric acid in it. Stir the mixture carefully. Add dry green tea leaves. Take a separate bowl and combine the olive oil, almond oil and tea tree oil in it together. Stir it carefully. Then combine the dry mixture and liquid mixture together. Stir the mixture carefully till you get nice mixture. You should get a slightly wet mixture. Then take the molds or muffins form and put the bath bomb mixture in it. Put the mixture in the molds very tight. Leave the bombs in a dry place for 6 hours. Then remove the bath bombs from the molds and keep in the cellophane bags.

# Anti-inflammatory bath bombs

## Thyme bath bomb

Thyme has antiseptic, anti-inflammatory, analgesic and antispasmodic properties. Also, it has a bronchodilator and expectorant action so that it can be used for the treatment of sore throats and bronchitis. The bath bombs with the dry thyme will help you to feel relaxed after a busy day.

**Directions**

1 teaspoon dry thyme
1 teaspoon pine essential oil
1 teaspoon olive oil
½ cup baking soda
1 cup salt
½ cup citric acid
1 tablespoon cornstarch
1 teaspoon rose essential oil

## Directions

Take the mixing bowl and place the dry thyme and pine essential oil in it. Stir the mixture with the help of the hand mixer. Then add olive oil and rose essential all. Take the spoon and stir the mixture very carefully. After this, start to add cornstarch, baking soda, and salt slowly. Whisk the mixture constantly. When you get a nice mixture – add citric acid. Stir it carefully again. Place the bath bomb mixture in the special bath bomb molds and press the mixture tightly. Leave the molds for 6 hours in a dry place. Then remove the bath bombs gently from the molds and wrap them in the wrapping paper. Keep the bath bombs in a dry place in your bathroom.

# Ginger bath bomb

The essential ginger oil has the ability to provide an anti-inflammatory and antiseptic effect. It is successfully used for the treatment of diseases of the nervous system and such diseases as arthritis, arthrosis, and different degrees of stretching. Essential oil improves memory, helps to get rid of fear, apathy, reduces aggression and causes a person to believe in themselves and their own strength. It also helps with headaches, migraines, and nausea caused by nerve disorders.

## Ingredients

1/3 cup baking soda
1 teaspoon dry ginger root
1 tablespoon essential ginger oil
1 teaspoon olive oil
2 tablespoon cornstarch
½ cup citric acid
1/3 cup salt
1 teaspoon sugar

## Directions

Take the big bowl and combine the olive oil and essential ginger oil in it. Then add dry ginger root and stir the mixture very carefully till you get nice mixture. Transfer the sugar to the oil mixture and stir it very carefully until the sugar is dissolved. Then take a separate bowl and combine the salt, baking soda, and citric acid in it. Add cornstarch and mix it up gently. Then pour the oil liquid in the dry mixture very slowly. Whisk it constantly. When you get a nice mixture – transfer it in the bath bomb molds and press them tightly. Leave the bath bomb molds for at least 8 hours. Then remove the bath bombs from the molds and use it. Keep the bath bombs in plastic bags in a dry place.

# Pine bath bomb

A special composition of essential oil of pine restores lung ventilation minimizes respiratory deficiency. It also regulates blood pressure, simplifies a migraine, relieves dizziness and eliminates from the tremor. Use the pine bath bombs when you catch a cold or just in the cold weather – it will help you feel better and sleep tight.

**Ingredients**

1 teaspoon essential pine oil
1 teaspoon olive oil
½ cup salt
1/3 cup citric acid
1 teaspoon ground cocoa beans
½ cup baking soda

**Directions**

Combine the salt, baking soda, and citric acid together in a mixing bowl. Add ground cocoa beans and stir the mixture carefully. Then pour olive oil in the mass and start to mix it slowly. When you get a smooth mass – add essential pine oil and stir the bath bomb mixture very carefully. After this, take the bath bomb molds or forms for muffins and put the mixture in it. Press the molds and leave them for at least 5 hours. Then remove the bath bombs from the molds and use them. Keep the bath bombs in the wrapping paper in a dry place.

# Rosemary bath bomb

Rosemary essential oil is used in case of problems with the respiratory tract, it relieves coughing.

The aroma of rosemary is considered as the "heart of the fragrance." It regulates the function of the circulatory system and the heart muscle and normalizes blood pressure. The rosemary has the ability to reduce the level of "bad" cholesterol in the blood, and have an anti-sclerotic effect.

## Ingredients

½ cup citric soda
1/3 cup baking soda
1 tablespoon starch
1 teaspoon rosemary essential oil
1 tablespoon almond oil
1 teaspoon dry rosemary

## Directions

Take the big mixing bowl and transfer the citric acid and baking soda in it. Add starch and stir the mixture carefully. Then add dry rosemary and stir the mass again. After this, take a separate mixing bowl and combine the rosemary essential oil and almond oil in it together. Whisk the mass. Then pour the liquid into the dry mixture very slowly. Stir it constantly till you get a smooth and nice mixture. Take the bath bomb's mold and put the mixture in it. Press it carefully and leave the bomb for 6 hours. Then remove the bomb from the mold and use it.

Keep the bath bombs in a dry place and the paper wrapping.

# Eucalyptus bath bomb

Eucalyptus essential oil is known as one of the most powerful agents against respiratory diseases.
The Eucalyptus essential oils used in dermatology for rashes on the skin and burns.

## Ingredients

½ cup citric acid
1/3 cup salt
2 tablespoon starch
1 teaspoon eucalyptus essential oil
1 teaspoon lemon tree oil
½ teaspoon peppermint oil
½ cup baking soda

## Directions

Take the big bowl and put the citric acid, baking soda and salt in it. Stir the mixture carefully. After this, add starch and stir it gently again. Then pour the peppermint oil in the dry mixture and start to whisk it till you get nice mixture. Take a separate bowl and combine the lemon tree oil and eucalyptus essential oil together in it. Stir it carefully. Then pour the oil mixture in the dry mass and continue to whisk it. When you get a slightly wet mixture - stop whisking it. Take the bath bomb forms or use a muffin pan and transfer the mixture to it. Put the mass very tightly. Then leave the forms with the bath bomb mixture in the dry and warm place for at least 4 hours. Remove the bath bombs from the forms and use it immediately or keep in the wrapping paper in the dry and warm place.

# Spearmint bath bomb

The spearmint bath bomb is the best way to feel calm after the difficult day. The spearmint is used to treat headaches, heart disease, nervous disorders, insomnia, asthma, gastric ulcer, colds, vomiting, throat diseases, kidney stones and liver, arteriosclerosis. Use the bath bomb for your evening time bath.

**Ingredients**

½ cup salt
¼ cup cream of tartar
1 cup citric acid
1 teaspoon spearmint essential oil
1 teaspoon almond oil
1 tablespoon olive oil
1 teaspoon dry spearmint leaves
½ cup baking soda

**Directions**

Take the big mixing bowl and combine salt, cream of tartar, baking soda and citric acid in it. Stir the mixture carefully. Take a separate bowl and combine the spearmint essential oil, almond oil, and olive oil in it. Whisk the mass. Then add dry spearmint leaves and stir it gently. After this, combine the liquid mixture and dry mixture together. Stir it carefully with the help of the spoon. Then transfer the mixture to the bath bomb's mold and press it tightly. Leave the bath bombs for at least 4 hours. Then remove the bath bombs from the molds and use it.
Keep the bath bombs in a dry place in the wrapped paper.

# Invigorating bath bomb

## Energy bath bomb

These bath bombs are the perfect solution for your morning procedure. The mix of the lemon and orange oil and will help you to wake up. Also, such mixture can fight with cellulite. The cinnamon and grapefruit oils will give you the feeling of cheerfulness for all day.

**Ingredients**

1 teaspoon essential orange oil
1 teaspoon essential lemon oil
½ teaspoon essential grapefruit oil
½ cup baking soda
1 teaspoon cinnamon oil
1 cup citric acid
½ cup salt
1 tablespoon cornstarch

**Directions**

Place the essential orange oil, the essential lemon oil, essential grapefruit oil, and cinnamon oil together in a mixing bowl. Mix it up gently. Then add the tablespoon of the cornstarch. After this, whisk the mixture carefully till you get a smooth mass. Then take a separate bowl and combine the dry ingredients in it (citric acid, baking soda, and salt). Stir the mixture little. Then pour the liquid mixture over the dry mixture and mix it with the help of the hand mixer. When you get a nice mixture – transfer it in the muffin's forms and press the mixture tightly into it. Leave the forms in a dry place for 5 hours. Then remove the bath bombs from the molds and wrap them in the cupboard bags. Keep the bath bombs in the dry and warm place.

# Lemon bath bombs

The essential lemon oil has the ability to slow down the action of the enzyme in the human body as elastase, which breaks down collagen and elastin fibers.

Therefore, the using of the essential lemon oil helps to extent slow down the aging of the skin, to prevent the appearance of wrinkles on the face. The lemon essential oil stimulates the growth of new skin cells and helps to smooth out existing wrinkles and improve the tone of already aging and sluggish skin. It is good for oily skin of the face because it normalizes sebum and helps to cleanse and narrow pores.

## Ingredients

1/3 cup baking soda
1 teaspoon essential lemon oil
½ teaspoon lemongrass oil
1 tablespoon olive oil
½ cup starch
1 cup citric acid
3 tablespoon sea salt
1 teaspoon dry lemon zest

## Directions

Take the mixing bowl and combine the essential lemon oil and olive oil together. Whisk the mixture gently with the help of the hand whisker. Then add lemongrass oil and lemon zest. Continue to whisk it and add starch. Stir the mixture till you get nice mixture. Then add citric acid and baking soda. Stir it carefully till you get a smooth mass. Then make the bath bombs from the mixture and transfer them to the plastic bags. Leave the bath bombs till them become dry. Then use them. Keep the bath bombs in a dry place in the bathroom.

# Mint and lime bath bomb

The usage of the mint oil is very well suited for oily skin. It was caused because of antiseptic, anti-inflammatory and antibacterial properties of the lemon oil. In particular, the mint oil helps to normalize the production of sebum and helps to narrow pores on the face.It can also be applied to eliminate acne.

## Ingredients

1 teaspoon dry mint
½ teaspoon dry lemon zest
1 teaspoon essential mint oil
½ teaspoon grape seed's oil
½ cup citric acid
½ cup salt
1/5 cup cornstarch
½ cup baking soda

## Directions

Place the liquid ingredients (essential mint oil and grape seed's oil) in a mixing bowl. Add cornstarch and stir the mixture very carefully with the help of the hand whisker. Then take a separate bowl and combine the dry lemon zest, baking soda, dry mint, citric acid, and salt together in it. Stir it gently. Then start to add liquid mixture to the dry mixture slowly. Stir it constantly. When you get a slightly wet mixture – place it in the special bath molds tightly. Leave the molds for at least 5 hours. Then remove the bath bombs from the molds and use them. Keep the bath bombs in a dry place in the cupboard bags.

# Grapefruit bath bomb

Grapefruit oil has a tonic and stimulating effect, works like an antidepressant. It has great antiseptic features. Grapefruit oil will help you to wake up in the morning and will help to avoid depression in the evening. Be careful with the grapefruit oil – do not use it much.

## Ingredients

1 teaspoon grapefruit oil
½ teaspoon essential orange oil
1 teaspoon almond oil
½ cup citric acid
½ cup salt
1 teaspoon starch
1 teaspoon dried grapefruit zest
1/3 cup baking soda

## Directions

Take the mixing bowl and combine the grapefruit zest and starch in it. Add essential orange oil and grapefruit oil. Stir it very carefully. After this, add citric acid, baking soda, and salt. Stir the mixture very carefully with the help of the spoon. When you get a nice mixture – add almond oil and continue to mix up the mixture. In the end, you will get little orange color mass. Take the bath bomb molds and transfer the mixture to them. Then press the bath bomb molds and leave them for 6 hours in a dry place. Then remove the bath bombs from the molds and use it. Keep the bath bombs in the wrapping paper in a dry place. Never keep the bath bombs in the bathroom.

# Lemongrass bath bomb

The bath bomb with the lemongrass is the best way to relax after the difficult day. The lemongrass oil has the great effect on the skin. It helps to keep in shape. The lemongrass oil is the best remedy for arthritis.

## Ingredients

1 tablespoon lemongrass oil
1 teaspoon cream of tartar
½ cup citric acid
1 cup salt
1 teaspoon hazel oil
1 teaspoon dry lemon leaves
1/3 cup baking soda

## Directions

Take the mixing bowl and combine the hazel oil and lemongrass oil together in it. Stir it gently and add dry lemon leaves. Leave the mass. After this, take a separate mixing bowl and combine the citric acid, baking soda, and salt in it. Stir it gently. Then pour the oil liquid in the dry mixture slowly. Stir it carefully till you get a nice mixture. Then add the cream of tartar and stir it again. You should get smooth and nice mixture. When the mixture is done – transfer it in the special bath bomb molds. Leave the bath bombs for 5 hours in a dry place. Then remove the "bombs" from the molds and wrap it in the wrapping paper. Keep the bath bombs in a dry place.

# Citrus bath bomb

Orange essential oil is suitable for all skin types. It normalizes its fat content, makes the skin supple and smooth, helps to avoid the wrinkles, relieves muscle tension. It also has bleaching properties, it helps lighten age spots. Displays toxins from the skin, and softens the rough skin. The citrus bath bomb is the best solution for your day bath.

## Ingredients

½ cup salt
½ cup baking soda
½ cup citric acid
1 tablespoon cornstarch
1 tablespoon orange essential oil
1 teaspoon dried orange zest
1 teaspoon coconut oil

## Directions

Combine the salt, citric acid, baking soda and cornstarch together in a mixing bowl. Stir it carefully. Take a separate mixing bowl and combine coconut oil, orange essential oil, and dried orange zest in it. Whisk the mixture till you get a smooth and nice mixture. Then combine the dry mixture and liquid mixture together in a mixing bowl. Stir it carefully with the help of the spoon. When you get a nice mixture – take the bath bomb's molds and transfer the mixture to it. Press it tightly. After this, leave the bath bombs in a dry place for 8 hours or overnight. When the bath bombs are done – remove them from the molds and wrap it in the wrapping paper.

# Skin softness bath bombs

## Honey bath bomb

The honey is rich in vitamins. It has an only positive influence on the human body. The honey has a pronounced antibacterial effect; it is effective as a diaphoretic. The people use honey for cure the heart disease and kidney disease. Be careful with honey it can cause the allergy.

**Ingredients**

½ cup baking soda
1 tablespoon honey
1 teaspoon olive oil
½ cup salt
½ cup citric acid
1 teaspoon cornstarch
1 teaspoon cinnamon
1 teaspoon dry lavender

**Directions**

Take the mixing bowl and combine the salt, baking soda, and citric acid in it. Mix up the mixture. Then combine the cornstarch, cinnamon, dry lavender, and honey together. Stir the mixture very carefully. After this, combine the liquid mixture and dry mixture together. Add olive oil. Then Stir the mixture with the help of the hand mixer. Stop to do it when you get a smooth mass. Then take the bath bomb molds and transfer the mixture to it. Press it carefully. Leave the bath bombs for 6 hours. Then remove the bath bombs from the molds and use them. Keep the bath bombs in the wrapping paper in a dry place.

# Macadamia bath bomb

Macadamia oil has can make the skin soft.  It has moisturizing, antioxidant, regenerating and rejuvenating properties. The Macadamia oil is well absorbed.
Macadamia oil can reduce the symptoms of a migraine, strengthen the immune system, angina, hinders the process of tumor formation. Anti-inflammatory properties of the oil make it an effective preventive measure against chronic diseases.

## Ingredients

1 tablespoon macadamia oil
½ cup citric acid
½ cup salt
1 teaspoon hazel oil
1 tablespoon cornstarch
¼ teaspoon cinnamon
½ cup baking soda

## Directions

Take the mixing bowl and combine the citric acid, baking soda, salt, and cornstarch in it. Stir the mixture gently and add cinnamon. Stir it again. After this, take the small mixing bowl and combine the hazel oil and macadamia oil in it. Whisk the liquid. Then pour the liquid slowly into the dry mixture. Stir the bath bomb mass very carefully till you get homogeneousconsistency. Then transfer the mass in the muffin forms and press it. Leave the bath bombs for 6 hours. Then remove the bath bombs from the forms and use it. Keep the bath bombs in plastic bags in a dry place.

# Jojoba oil bomb

The jojoba oil makes any type of skin better and feels younger. It has aparticularly beneficial effect on inflamed it, over-dried and peeling skin. Tired, fading and loose skin also needs this oil, it helps get rid of wrinkles and fine cracks. Such bath bombs will be a great solution for all types of skin. Use the bath bombs for your evening bath.

## Ingredients

1 tablespoon jojoba oil
1 teaspoon dry lavender
½ cup citric acid
1 cup salt
½ teaspoon almond oil
½ cup baking soda

## Directions

Take the mixing bowl and combine the jojoba oil and almond oil in it. Stir the mixture carefully and add dry lavender. Stir it again. Then combine the citric acid, baking soda and salt together. Stir it gently. Pour the liquid mixture over the dry mixture slowly and stir the mass. When you get a smooth and nice mixture – the mixture is done. Transfer it in the bath bomb molds or just use the forms for muffins and leave them in a warm place for 4 hours. Then remove the bath bombs from the molds and keep them in the cupboard bags in a warm and dry place.

# Himalayan pink salt bath bomb

Shea butter is a source of vitamins A and E that are necessary for the normal condition of the skin.

Vitamin A promotes regeneration (renewal) cells, making the skin rejuvenated. Also, vitamin A effectively soothes and nourishes dry, acne, and skin gaunt.

Vitamin E slows the aging process and reduces the risk of cancer cells due to its antioxidant properties, improves microcirculation.

## Ingredients

½ cup Himalayan pink salt
½ cup citric acid
1/3 cup salt
1 teaspoon coconut oil
1 tablespoon Shi butter
½ teaspoon almond oil
½ cup baking soda

## Directions

Make the dry base: take the big mixing bowl and combine the Himalayan pink salt, baking soda, citric acid, and salt together. Stir the mixture carefully with the help of the spoon. Then take a separate bowl and combine almond oil and coconut oil together. Whisk it. Combine the dry mixture and liquid mixture together. Stir the mixture till you get nice mixture. After this, add Shi butter and stir it gently. You should get plastic mass. Take some mixture in the hands and make the balls with the help of the palms. Then transfer the bombs in the forms and leave them for 5 hours. Then remove the bath bombs from the molds and keep them in the plastic paper in a dry place.

# Epsom salt and coconut oil bath bomb

The coconut oil helps to preserve skin moisture and restore the barrier function of the epidermis, prevents the accumulation of fat in the body. It helps to restore the acid-alkaline balance of the skin and improves the oxygenation of the skin.

## Ingredients

1 cup Epsom salt
1 tablespoon coconut oil
½ cup citric acid
1 tablespoon cornstarch
½ teaspoon vanilla essential oil
½ cup baking soda

## Directions

Make the liquid base for the bath bomb: combine the coconut oil and vanilla essential oil together. Whisk the mixture. Then take a separate bowl and make the dry mixture. Combine the Epsom salt, citric acid, baking soda, and cornstarch together. Stir the mixture with the help of the spoon. Then pour the liquid mixture into the dry mixture. Stir the mixture very carefully. Use the hand for this step. In the end, you should get a slightly wet mixture. Transfer the bath bomb mixture in the special forms and leave them for at least 5 hours. Then remove the bath bombs from the forms and wrap it in the paper wrapping. Keep the bath bombs in the cupboard bags.

# Cocoa oil bomb

The cocoa oil can help to protect your skin from the cold influence. The cocoa oil is the best for the face. It is great for dry, flaky, and exhausted skin with insufficient moisture.
Cocoa butter nourishes, moisturizes, softens, revitalizes and tones the skin, making it more soft, smooth and radiant. In addition, it has smoothing properties.

## Ingredients

1 tablespoon cocoa butter
½ teaspoon coconut oil
½ cup salt
1 cup citric acid
1 teaspoon starch
½ teaspoon cocoa powder
1/3 cup baking soda

## Directions

Take the bowl and combine the cocoa butter and coconut oil in it. Stir it carefully and then whisk the mass with the help of the hand whisker. Take the mixing bowl and combine the salt, baking soda, citric acid, starch, and cocoa powder in it. Stir it carefully. After this, combine the dry mixture and liquid mixture together. Stir it carefully. Then transfer the mass in the muffins forms and press it a little. Leave the forms with the bath bomb mixture for 6 hours or overnight in a dry place. Then remove the bath bombs from the forms and use it. Keep the bath bombs in a dry place in cupboard bags.

# Bath bomb with Vitamin E

Vitamin E protects the skin from ultraviolet radiation. The vitamin E prevents the skin from damage by UV light. The vitamin E makes the skin feel better. It makes it soft and smooth. Use the bath bombs with the Vitamin E for your day bath.

## Ingredients

1/3 tablespoon vitamin E
1 tablespoon Shi butter
1 teaspoon olive oil
½ cup citric acid
½ cup salt
1 tablespoon cornstarch
1 teaspoon coconut
½ cup baking soda

## Directions

Take the medium mixing bowl and put citric acid, baking soda and salt in it. Stir it carefully and add vitamin E slowly. Stir the mixture carefully and add coconut. Stir it again till you get nice mixture. Then take a separate bowl and combine the olive oil, Shi butter and cornstarch in it. Whisk the mixture till you get fluffy mass. Then combine the dry and liquid mixture together and stir it carefully. Take the bath bomb's mold and transfer the mass to it. Press it a little. Leave the mold with the bath bomb mixture for at least 4 hours in a dry place. Then remove the bombs from the molds and wrap it in the paper. Keep in warm but dry place.

# Olive oil bath bomb

The olive oil has softening, moisturizing and antiseptic properties and can be used for body and face. It is rich in calcium, iron, copper, and vitamins A, D and E. Some drops of olive oil will have to make your skin soft and fluffy.

## Ingredients

1 tablespoon olive oil
½ teaspoon almond oil
1 teaspoon lavender
1 cup citric acid
½ cup salt
2 tablespoon cornstarch
1/3 cup baking soda

## Directions

Take the bowl and combine the cornstarch and almond oil in it. Then pour olive oil in the mixture and stir it carefully till you get a smooth, nice mixture. Then take a separate mixing bowl and combine the citric acid, baking soda and salt together in it. Stir the mixture. Then combine the oil mixture and dry mixture together. Mix it carefully with the help of the hand mixer. When you get a nice mixture – transfer it in the special bath bomb molds. Leave the bath bombs for 5 hours in a dry place. Then remove them from the molds and keep them in a dry place in the cupboard bags.

# Cotton bath bomb

The unique properties represented by cotton oil help to stabilize the lipid balance of the skin through its moisturizing and effective recovery. The cotton oil has protected features that can help to care for body and face. The cotton bath bomb will be a great decision for an every day bath.

## Ingredients

1 tablespoon cotton oil
1 teaspoon almond oil
1 cup salt
½ cup citric acid
2 tablespoon cornstarch
½ cup baking soda

## Directions

Take the mixing bowl and combine the cornstarch, baking soda, citric acid, and salt in it. Stir the mixture. Then pour the cotton oil in the dry mixture. Stir it gently and add almond oil. Take the hand mixer and mix the mixture till you get a smooth mass. After this, take the bath bomb molds and transfer the mixture to them.  Put the mixture every tightly. Then leave the molds for 6-8 hours in a dry place. When the bath bombs are dry – remove them from the molds and use them. Keep the bath bombs in a dry place in the cupboard bags.

# Cinnamon bath bomb

The cinnamon has not only so delicious smell but also very useful for our body. The cinnamon due to its constituent vitamins, antioxidants, trace elements improves skin and hair. Regular use the cinnamon for your body will improve skin color (pale to eliminate), clean the pores, activate blood circulation and metabolism, smooth out wrinkles fine mesh. Caring products for hair with cinnamon enhance growth and strengthen the hair along the entire length.

**Ingredients**

2 tablespoon cinnamon
1 cup salt
1 cup citric acid
1 teaspoon cornstarch
1 teaspoon olive oil
1 teaspoon almond oil
1 teaspoon essential jasmine oil
½ cup baking soda

**Directions**

Combine the cornstarch, baking soda, and citric acid together in a mixing bowl. Then add salt and cinnamon. Stir the mixture very carefully with the help of the fork. After this take a separate bowl and combine the olive oil, essential jasmine oil, and almond oil together. Stir it carefully and pour it slowly in the dry mixture. Stir it constantly. Then make the bath bombs from the mixture and transfer them into the special bath bombs molds. Leave the bath bombs for at least 5 hours and then remove the bath bombs. Keep the bath bombs in a dry place. Wrap them in the wrapping paper.

# Almond oil bath bomb

The almond oil helps to improve the complexion and skin tone, giving it a healthy glow. Also, oil is widely used to lighten the skin, and regular use cleanses the skin, leaving it soft and supple.

Skin diseases such as psoriasis and eczema, which causes inflammation of the skin, as well as redness, itching and rash can be decreased by using almond oil. Topical application of almond oil can temporarily relieve the inflammation and irritation. Almond oil can act as an allergen and cause skin irritation.

## Ingredients

1/2 cup baking soda
1 tablespoon almond oil
1 teaspoon olive oil
½ cup citric acid
½ cup salt
2 tablespoon cornstarch

## Directions

Take the mixing bowl and combine the almond oil and olive oil together. Stir the mixture. Then add salt, baking soda, and cornstarch. Stir the mixture. Then start to add citric acid. Do it very slowly and stir the mixture constantly. Mix it up with the help of the hand mixer. When you get a nice mixture – transfer the mixture in the bath bomb molds or use muffins molds for it. Leave the bath bombs in adry place for at least 7 hours. Then remove the bath bombs from the molds and use it. Keep the bath bombs in plastic bags.

# Detox bath bomb

The mix of the essential oil can make you feel better and avoid the toxic influence of the atmosphere. Such essential oils as orange oil, cardamom oil, and jojoba oil will help you not only feel relaxed but will care about your skin – will make it soft.

## Ingredients

1 teaspoon jojoba oil
1 teaspoon eucalyptus essential oil
1 teaspoon olive oil
1 teaspoon cardamom oil
½ teaspoon essential orange oil
1 cup salt
1 cup citric acid
2 tablespoon cornstarch
½ cup baking soda

## Directions

Take the big mixing bowl and combine the jojoba oil, eucalyptus essential oil, and olive oil together. Take the hand whisker and whisk the mixture carefully. Then add cardamom oil and essential orange oil. Continue to whisk the mixture for 30 seconds more. Then add salt, baking soda, and cornstarch. Stir the mixture and when you get a nice mixture – add citric acid. Stir the mass carefully again. Then take the bath bomb molds and transfer the mixture to them.  Press the molds and leave them for 7 hours. When the bath bombs are dry – remove them from the molds and wrap then in the wrapping paper. Keep the bath bombs in a dry place.

# Coffee bath bomb

The coffee has tightened effect, it tones the skin, nourishes. It can nurture the skin by coffee oils, improves color and, of course, helps to effectively fight cellulite. The Coffee Body Scrub has unique cosmetic properties – it can make your skin soft and fluffy.

## Ingredients

½ cup baking soda
1 tablespoon ground coffee
1 teaspoon essential coffee oil
½ cup salt
½ cup citric acid
3 tablespoon cornstarch
1 tablespoon olive oil
1 teaspoon essential vanilla oil

## Directions

Mix up the essential vanilla oil and ground coffee. Then add essential coffee oil. Stir the mixture. After this, combine the salt, baking soda, and olive oil together. Add the cornstarch and stir the mixture carefully. Then add essential vanilla oil mixture in the salt mixture and mix it up carefully with the help of the spoon. When you get a smooth mixture – add citric acid. Never add the citric acid before you get a nice mixture – otherwise, it can damage the fizzy features of the bath bombs. Then transfer the bath bomb mixture in the special molds and leave them at least 6 hours. Then remove the bath bombs from the molds and wrap them in the wrapping paper. Keep the bath bombs in a dry place.

# Milk and honey bath bomb

Honey and milk - are multifunctional tools that will help to solve any problems of the skin. It is impossible to overestimate the useful features of this mixture. It can be applied on the skin of any type and of any age. The bath bombs with honey and milk can make your skin feel younger and softer. Such bath bombs are useful at any time of the day. It will make you feel full of energy during morning bath and calm – during night or evening bath.

## Ingredients

½ cup baking soda
½ cup citric acid
1 cup salt
4 tablespoon dry milk
1 teaspoon liquid honey
1 teaspoon bee propolis
1 teaspoon almond oil
1 teaspoon olive oil
1 teaspoon Shi butter

## Directions

Take the big bowl and combine the dry milk and liquid honey in it. Add salt, baking soda, and bee propolis. Start to mix the mixture with the help of the hand mixer. Then add almond oil, olive oil, and Shi butter. Stir the mixture for 1 minute more. Then add citric acid. Stir it carefully again and when you get the nice mixture – make the bath bombs. Then transfer the bath bombs in the special molds and press them tightly. Leave the bath bombs for 6 hours in a dry place. Then remove the bath bombs from the molds and keep them in the wrapping paper.

# Oatmeal bath bomb

The oatmeal is very useful for our skin. It nourishes the skin and makes it soft and fluffy.
The benefits of oatmeal are caused by its anti-inflammatory and antioxidant properties, which have an anti-aging effect on the skin. The bath bombs with the oatmeal and olive oil will give you the feeling of lightness and softness.

## Ingredients

1/3 cup baking soda
1/3 cup oatmeal
½ cup salt
1 cup citric acid
1 teaspoon cornstarch
2 tablespoon olive oil

## Directions

Combine the oatmeal, baking soda, and salt together in a mixing bowl. Add cornstarch. Then start to add olive oil slowly. Whisk the mixture constantly. Then add citric acid. Stir the mass with the help of the spoon. When the mixture becomes smooth and slightly wet – transfer it in the bath bomb molds. Press them a little and leave them in the dry and warm place for 4 hours. Then remove the bath bombs from the molds and pack them in the plastic or cupboard bags. Keep the bath bombs in the bathroom in a dry place.

# Pumpkin spicy bath bomb

The pumpkin oil contains large amounts of polyunsaturated fatty acids, vitamins, and important for our skin minerals. One of the main features of the pumpkin oil is its possibility to slow down the aging process. It is well-known oil that is wide used in the cosmetology.

The pumpkin oil is well suited for dry, dehydrated and mature skin rough, which is caused by its effective regenerating, moisturizing, nourishing and rejuvenating effect.

## Ingredients

1 tablespoon pumpkin oil
1 teaspoon cinnamon
1 teaspoon vanilla essential oil
1 cup cornstarch
1 cup citric acid
1/3 cup sea salt
½ cup baking soda

## Directions

Combine the cornstarch and pumpkin oil. Stir the mixture very carefully with the help of the hand whisker. Then add cinnamon, baking soda, and vanilla essential oil. Stir the mixture gently. After this, add salt. When you get a smooth and a slightly wet mixture – add citric acid. Take the spoon and churn the mass till you get a smooth mass. Then transfer the mixture in the special bath bomb molds or use muffin form for this step. Put the mixture very tightly in the molds. Leave the molds for at least 4 hours in a warm place. Then remove the bath bombs from the forms and use it. Keep the bath bombs in the wrapping paper in a dry place.

# Achy muscles bath bomb

A mix of oils and arrowroot powder will help to relax your achy muscles. The Shi butter makes the skin soft and nourishes it. Such bath bombs are the best for evening time bath. Use it at least 2 times per week.

## Ingredients

1 teaspoon arrowroot powder
½ cup baking soda
1/3 cup citric acid
½ cup sea salt
1 teaspoon almond oil
1 teaspoon Shi butter
1 teaspoon cocoa oil

## Directions

Place the citric acid, baking soda and salt in a mixing bowl and stir the mixture gently. Then combine the almond oil, Shi butter and cocoa oil in a separate boil. Stir the mixture with the help of the hand mixer. After this, add arrowroot powder and continue to mix it for 30 seconds more. Then pour the liquid mixture in the dry mixture slowly. Stir it carefully will you get nice mixture. Then transfer the bath bomb mixture in the special bath bomb molds and press it tightly. Leave the bath bombs for 5 hours then remove them from the molds and wrap them in the wrapping paper. Keep the bath bombs in a dry place.

## Rosehip bath bomb

The rosehip oil is the best oil for all types of the skin. It has a positive influence on the dry skin – makes it softer. Every day using the rosehip oil can help you to avoid the pigment spots.

**Ingredients**

1 teaspoon dry rosehip
½ cup baking soda
1 teaspoon olive oil
1 teaspoon rosehip oil
1/4cup oatmeal
½ cup starch
½ cup Epsom salt
1 teaspoon sweet almond oil
½ cup citric acid

**Directions**

Put the dry rosehip in a mixing bowl and add olive oil. Stir it gently and leave the mixture. Then take a separate bowl and combine the Epsom salt, baking soda,starch, and oatmeal in it. Stir the mixture and add citric acid. After this, combine the rosehip mixture and dry mixture together. Add sweet almond oil and rosehip oil. Whisk the mixture with the help of the hand whisker for this step. When you get a nice mixture – transfer the mixture in the special bath bomb molds and press them tightly. Then remove the bath bombs from the molds and leave them in a dry place for at least 7 hours. After this, wrap the bath bombs in the wrapping paper and keep them in a dry place.

# Ylang-Ylang bath bomb

The essential oil of ylang-ylang prevents the premature aging of the skin, as well as to get rid of acne. Essential oil of ylang-ylang in the deep layers of the skin acts by activating the growth of new cells and giving the skin elasticity, soft and velvety. It can remove the irritation and redness of the skin problem. The oil is widely used to treat dermatitis and eczema; it also contributes to the restoration of thin and brittle hair prone to hair loss.

## Ingredients

1 teaspoon essential ylang-ylang oil
1 teaspoon jasmine oil
½ tablespoon olive oil
1 teaspoon dry chamomile
½ teaspoon dry daisy
½ cup Epsom salt
½ cup baking soda
½ cup citric acid

## Directions

Place the essential ylang-ylang oil and jasmine oil together in a mixing bowl. Add olive oil and dry chamomile. Stir the mixture carefully. Then add dry daisy and stir the mixture again. After this, take a separate bowl and combine the Epsom salt, baking soda, and citric acid in it together. Stir the mixture. Pour the liquid mixture over the dry mixture slowly. Stir it carefully. When you get a smooth and nice mixture - transfer it in the special bath bomb molds. Press the mixture tightly. Leave the bath bombs for 5 hours in a dry place. Then remove the bath bombs from the molds and wrap them in the wrapping paper. Keep in a dry place.

# Calendula bath bomb

The calendula essential oil is rich in, fatty acids, carotene, volatile, vitamin C, and bitter substances. It has a powerful anti-inflammatory effect. Calendula oil is an excellent remedy for inflamed skin, and acne. Such bath bombs will be useful for you if you have some problems with skin.

**Ingredients**

1 teaspoon dry calendula
1 teaspoon essential calendula oil
½ cup baking soda
1 teaspoon olive oil
½ cup citric acid
3 tablespoon cornstarch
1 cup salt

**Directions**

Combine the dry calendula with the cornstarch and salt. Stir the mixture carefully. Then add olive oil and essential calendula oil. Stir the mixture carefully. Then use the hand mixer to make the smooth mass. Start to add citric acid, baking soda, and continue to Stir the mixture with the help of the mixer. When you get a nice mixture – transfer it in the bath bomb molds and press the mixture tightly. Leave the bath bombs for 5 hours in a dry place. Then remove the bath bombs from the molds and use them. Keep the bath bombs in plastic bags in a dry place or in the bathroom.

# Chocolate bath bomb

The structure of chocolate includes theobromine and theophylline. These agents activate a group of biochemical reactions in the skin, providing a lifting effect. One more important feature is its sweet treats saturation micronutrients such as iron, copper, magnesium, which are necessary for the occurrence of many reactions and serve to maintain the normal activity of the skin.

## Ingredients

1 tablespoon dry milk
1 teaspoon cocoa essential oil
½ cup baking soda
1 teaspoon chocolate flakes
1 cup salt
½ cup citric acid
1 teaspoon cinnamon oil

## Directions

Place the dry milk in a mixing bowl and add essential cocoa oil. Then mince the chocolate flakes and add them to the dry milk mixture. Stir the mass very carefully with the help of the hand whisker. Then add cinnamon oil and salt. Mix up the mixture. After this, add citric acid, baking soda, and continue to whisk it till you get a smooth and nice mixture. Then transfer the mixture in the bath bomb molds and press them tightly. Leave the bath bombs for at least 7 hours. Then remove them from the bath bomb molds. Keep the done bath bombs in a dry place in the wrapping paper or plastic bags.

# Peach bath bomb

The peach oil contains carotenoids (organic pigments give color to the fruit) and minerals: phosphorus, potassium, iron and calcium. All these features help to rejuvenate and strengthen the skin. The peach oil has antioxidant properties that are invaluable in property issues of slowing aging.

## Ingredients

1 tablespoon peach oil
1 tablespoon cornstarch
1 teaspoon cinnamon
½ teaspoon minced grape seeds
1/3 cup baking soda
½ cup salt
½ cup citric acid
1 teaspoon ylang-ylang oil

## Directions

Take the small mixing bowl and combine the peach oil and ylang-ylang oil in it. Stir the mixture gently. Then add minced grape seeds and cornstarch. Stir the mixture very carefully till you get nice mixture. Then combine the citric acid, baking soda, salt, and cinnamon together. Stir the mixture. Pour the liquid oil mixture in the citric acid mass. Whisk it carefully till you get a smooth mass. Then place the bath bomb mixture in the plastic bath bomb molds and press them tightly. Leave the bath bomb molds for 6 hours in a dry place. Then remove the bath bombs from them and wrap the in the wrapping paper. Keep the bath bombs in the bathroom in a dry place.

# Grape seed's bath bomb

The grape seed's oil is suitable for oily and combination skin; it has the ability to reduce sebum secretion and tighten the pores without clogging them. Oil is easily absorbed into the skin and gives it a natural healthy color.

Grape seed oil has a strong moisturizing, regenerating, antioxidant and vitaminizing action. It is used to restore the elasticity of aging skin in the neck; it is useful for weight loss. With its tonic properties, oil is effective for cellulite; it helps to get rid of rosacea, varicose veins, making blood vessel walls more elastic, activating circulation.

## Ingredients

1 teaspoon grape seed's oil
1 teaspoon grape seeds
½ cup baking soda
1 tablespoon oatmeal
1 teaspoon cornstarch
½ cup citric acid
½ cup salt
1 teaspoon olive oil

## Directions

Combine the grape seeds and oatmeal together. Then add salt, baking soda, and citric acid. Stir the mixture carefully. After this, take the small mixing bowl and combine the olive oil, grape seed's oil and cornstarch together. Whisk the mixture with the help of the hand whisker. Then pour the liquid into the dry mixture. Use hands to mix up the mixture. At the end, you should get smooth and nice mixture. Then place the mixture in the special bath bomb molds or use the muffins forms for this procedure. Leave them for 6 hours. When the time is running out – remove the bath bombs from the molds and wrap them in plastic bags. Keep the bath bombs in a dry place.

# The Dead Sea mud bath bomb

Dead Sea mud can deal with skin ailments, nervous and cardiovascular systems, digestive, respiratory, renal, musculoskeletal system; mud helps to cope with women's and men's issues, as well as endocrine disorders.

## Ingredients

1 tablespoon the Dead Sea dry mud
½ cup the Dead Sea salt
½ cup baking soda
½ cup citric acid
1 tablespoon olive oil
1 teaspoon sweet almond oil

## Directions

Take the big mixing bowl and combine Dead Sea salt, mud, baking soda, and citric acid together in it. Stir the mixture. After this, pour the olive oil in the mixture and start to stir it carefully with the help of the spoon. Then add sweet almond oil and whisk the mixture. When you get little-wet mixture – transfer it in the special bath bomb's molds and press the mixture carefully in the molds. Leave the bath bombs for 7 hours. After this, remove the bath bombs from the molds and wrap them in plastic bags. Keep the bath bombs in a dry place.

# Castor oil bath bomb

The oil is primarily used as a nutritional agent for dry skin. It has very strong soft effect; it helps to cope with such skin problems like dryness, lack of moisture, scaling, roughness, unevenness and loss of elasticity of the skin.

Castor oil also can be an excellent emollient and soothing agent for the care of sensitive skin. But sometimes it can cause allergic reactions of the skin.

## Ingredients

1 tablespoon castor oil
1 teaspoon cinnamon oil
1/3 cup baking soda
1 teaspoon olive oil
½ cup citric acid
1/3 cup salt
4 tablespoon cornstarch

## Directions

Place the castor oil, cinnamon oil, and olive oil together in a mixing bowl. Mix up the mixture. Then add cornstarch and baking soda, and stir the mass carefully again till you get a smooth and nice mixture. After this, take a separate big mixing bowl and combine the citric acid and salt in it. Mix up the dry mass. Then pour the oil mixture in the dry mass. Whisk it constantly. Stir the mixture till you get a smooth and nice mixture. After this, place the mass in the special bath bomb mold and press it a little. Leave the bath bombs for at least 4 hours. Then remove them from the molds and wrap them in the wrapping paper. Keep the bath bombs in the bathroom in a dry place.

## Avocado oil bath bomb

Oil avocado contains a complex of fatty acids, which are directly involved in the development of human cells and normalize blood flow. The avocado oil is also necessary to adjust the fat metabolism and removes toxins, radionuclides, and heavy metals.

### Ingredients

1 teaspoon avocado oil
½ cup baking soda
1 teaspoon thyme oil
1 tablespoon cornstarch
½ cup citric acid
¼ cup Epsom salt
1 teaspoon dry lemon zest

### Directions

Place the cornstarch, baking soda, citric acid, and Epsom salt together in a mixing bowl. Stir the mixture. Then add dry lemon zest and stir it again gently. Take a separate mixing bowl and pour thyme oil and avocado oil in it. Mix up the mass. After this, pour the liquid mixture into the dry mixture and whisk it constantly. Continue to whisk the mass till you get a smooth and nice mixture. Then take the muffin molds and place the bath bomb mixture in them. Press the mixture in the molds tightly. Then leave the muffin's molds for at least 6 hours. After this, remove the bath bombs from the molds and wrap them in the wrapping paper. Keep the bath bombs in a dry place in the bathroom.

# If you enjoyed this book, don't forget to leave

# a review on Amazon! I highly appreciate

# your reviews, and it only takes a minute to

# do.

### Your Free Gift

I wanted to show my appreciation that you support my work so I've put together a free gift for you.

http://www.olkha.co/gelato.html

Gelato - Italian-style ice cream cookbook

Just visit the link above to download it now.

I know you will love this gift.

Thanks!


## Other books from the series

50 *Beauty* RECIPES

HOMEMADE LOTIONS AND CREAMS! JUST 15 MINUTES TO BE NATURAL & STAY ORGANIC

+FREE GIFT INSIDE

Nora Robson

https://www.amazon.com/dp/B01N1OD108

23265197R00037

Printed in Great Britain
by Amazon